The Rise of ISIS

The Threat Of ISIS and The Origins of ISIS Explained

Copyright ©

Disclaimer

All the material contained in this book is provided for educational and informational purposes only. No responsibility can be taken for any results or outcomes resulting from the use of this material.

While every attempt has been made to provide information that is both accurate and effective, the author does not assume any responsibility for the accuracy or use/misuse of this information.

Table of Contents

Chapter 1 Acts Of Terror

Chapter 2 How ISIS Came To Be

Chapter 3 Key ISIS Personalities

Chapter 4. Brutal Propaganda

Chapter 5. The Treatment of Women And Children Under ISIS

Chapter 6. Why Isis Is Thriving

Chapter 1 Acts Of Terror

The recent Charlie Hebdo attack is an example of terrorism that has struck at the hearts of many. Some of the worst acts of terrorism that have been committed during this generation's lifetime include the Lockerbie Bombing of 1988 which claimed the lives of 270 people supposedly perpetuated by a couple of Libyan nationals, the loss of between 200 to 400 people from the Benthala village at the hands of the Armed Islamic Group back in 1997, and the Madrid Train Bombings of 2004 wherein almost 200 people perished.

Also in 2004, 116 lives were lost in what is considered the deadliest terrorist attack at sea when the Abu Sayyaf Group in the Philippines attacked a ferry. The lives of 209 people were lost while 714 more were injured during the bombing of the Mumbai Suburban Railway by the Lashkar-e-Toba and the Students Islamic Movement of India or SIMI.

Another terrorist group that is spreading fear nowadays is Boko Haram, which is an Islamist movement in Nigeria. Boko Haram is responsible for the death of possibly more than 5,000 people in Nigeria, Cameroon, and Chad. They are also behind the abduction of 276 girls from a Chibok school in 2014.

Of course who could ever forget the most devastating terrorist act in recent memory – the 9/11 attack. On that fateful day of September 11, 2001, more than 3,000 lives were lost after four attacks by the al-Queda using hijacked passenger planes. What makes this act more devastating is that it targeted the United States, considered one of the superpowers of the world. We all know what happened next. An all-out war against the perpetrators and other militant extremist organizations was conducted. The War on Terror is highlighted by the assassination of Osama Bin Laden, the leader of the Taliban group responsible for the 9/11 attacks, at the hands of the US Navy S.E.A.L. Team 6. This was during a covert Pakistani mission which was later the basis for the movie Zero Dark Thirty starring Jessica Chastain.

Other highlights of the still ongoing War On Terror was the toppling of Saddam Hussein's government in 2003 and the execution of Iraq's dictator three years later, the War in Afghanistan, the War in North-West Pakistan, and the Insurgency in Yemen. Suffice to say, since the United States under the administration of then-President George W. Bush, and other NATO and non-NATO forces started the Global War on Terrorism, scores of men and women, from all sides have lost their lives. Even more disturbing is that innocent lives, including those of children, have been sacrificed.

Sadly, the death of Hussein and Bin Laden did not prevent other personalities and groups from orchestrating other acts of terrorism. At the forefront of numerous terroristic and simply brutal acts that got our attention the past couple of years is the group known as ISIS. Not all terrorist attacks entail bombings and massacres. Terrorism is defined as any violent action with the purpose of instilling fear. This makes the succession of executions that has been discussed in numerous news programs and can be viewed in videos downloaded in the Internet as terroristic actions. The group behind these brutal executions is known as ISIS which is not to be confused with the Ancient Greek goddess of health, marriage and wisdom.

ISIS or the Islamic State of Iraq and Syria was virtually unknown to most of us until recently after it introduced itself to the world in the most dastardly way – holding an innocent journalist hostage and then executing him for all the world to see. However, the group has been one of the targets of the War on Terror for years. Ever since the name ISIS which is also called ISIL for Islamic State of Iraq and Levant came up, not a few wondered who they are and what are they supposedly championing for. Of course the question of how they came to be was begging to be answered.

Chapter 2 How ISIS Came To Be

The answer may lie in Bucca. According to some reports, the American detention facility in Iraq known as Camp Bucca may be the catalyst for the strengthening of the ISIS terrorist group. Ever since the US and other countries fought the insurgents, more and more prisoners were taken, even numbering well over a hundred thousand. Many of them were held in Camp Bucca in Qasr. It is believed that it was here that the main proponents of ISIS became more than fellow inmates.

The top leaders of ISIS were all former inmates in Camp Bucca which became the reason why they met and shared ideologies and grievances. Inmates who were loyal to Saddam Hussein, the Ba'athists, came into contact with members of different Islamic extremist groups paving the way for an alliance that whose power is being felt now.

Suffice to say, having a common foe in the NATO forces and having similar beliefs led the formation of ISIS. Additionally, more and more prisoners were becoming radicalized. One of which would be the future leader of ISIS or ISIL. American authorities later admitted that they did notice something was brewing inside the prison camp. A rehabilitation program proved useless in this scenario as it was either ineffective or was not properly implemented. The American government's focus on squashing the insurgencies and creating a new Iraq government may have led to this "new" threat to everybody's peaceful existence.

ISIS was actually established back in 1999 paving the way for some to wonder why they only heard about them in recent years. This is mostly because the group was originally known as Jamā'at al-Tawḥīd wa-al-Jihad, which is rather hard to pronounce much more remember. It held this name until 2004 when they became part of the al-Qaeda group. It then changed its name to Tanzim Qaidat al-Jihad fi Bilad al-Rafidaynthough they were better known as al-Qaeda in Iraq or AQI. In 2006, the AQI along with other Sunni insurgents formed the Islamic State of Iraq or ISI. In 2013, they became known as ISIS or ISIL after the group laid claim to Syria and Levant.

The ISIS is believed to be responsible for Turkey's deadliest single act of terrorism which happened on the 11th of May. They detonated two car bombs in the Hatay Province particularly in Reyhanli where more than 50 people were killed that day while 140 more were injured from the blasts. Two months later, Abu Bassir Al-Jeblawi of the Free Syrian Army was killed. The battalion chief, whose real name was Kamal Hamami, was on his way to the Al-Izz Bin Abdulsalam brigade when he passed by members of the ISIS group who later killed him.

The United Nations has officially designated ISIS or ISIL as a terrorist group. Thanks in large part to the scores of lives the group have claimed in the name of "ethnic cleansing". They are also involved in countless war crimes and human rights abuses.

Chapter 3 Key ISIS Personalities

Abu Bakr al-Baghdadi

The self-proclaimed Islamic State is led by Abu Bakr al-Baghdadi, the man mentioned earlier. Also called Abu Du'a, Abu Bakr Al-Baghdadi Al-Husseini Al-Qurashi, and Amir al-Mu'minin, the ISIL leader was born in 1971 somewhere near Samarra, Iraq. He was said to be a shy and religious youngster during his adolescent years with his being a football aficionado probably his most striking quality.

Baghdadi went on to become a scholar and earned a doctorate in Islamic studies from either the Islamic University in Baghdad or from the University of Baghdad. He was described as a loner and somewhat insignificant by the leader of the Islamic Army of Iraq, Ahmed al-Dabash, who happened to be studying the same course as Baghdadi. The ISIL leader is such a mystery that the man born as Ibrahim Awad Ibrahim al-Badri has been called "the invisible sheikh" by those who fight for him and their Islamic State.

The reasons why and how Baghdadi turned from an insignificant young lad to the leader of one of the most brutal jihadist groups to date is still up in the air. There are those who stress that Baghdadi was a simple mosque cleric while others disagree and point out that he was already an insurgent during Saddam Hussein's rule. One thing analysts agree on is that Baghdadi was the brain behind Jamaat Jaysh Ahl al-

Sunnah wa-l-Jamaah or JJASJ, another militant group. In 2006, his group became part of the Mujahideen Shura Council or MSC. During his time with the MSC, Baghdadi was appointed as part of its sharia committee. During the same year, MSC changed its name to the Islamic State of Iraq or ISI which is the predecessor of ISIS and ISIL.

Baghdadi also served in the ISI's sharia committee, this time as the general supervisor. The future ISIS leader was said to have been imprisoned in Camp Bucca for a still undetermined crime. This allowed him to rub shoulders with radicals and extremists in the same camp. As fate would have it, the formerly nerdy Baghdadi would see himself rise in ranks and become one of the most wanted men in the world.

Abu Muslim al-Turkmani

Abu Muslim al-Turkmani , whose real name was Fadel Ahmed Abdullah al-Hiyali, is another high-ranking personality in the group. Al-Turkmani who acted as the Deputy leader in Iraq while he was still alive was killed during an airstrike on November or December 2014. He was in charge of military operations while also overseeing the local councils in Iraq. The late Al-Turkmani's counterpart in Syria is Abu Ali al-Anbari. What Al-Turkmani did in Iraq, al-Anbari did in Syria. Al-Anbari served under the late strongman Saddam Hussein as a Major General of the Iraqi Army.

Abu Ayman al-Iraqi

Abu Ayman al-Iraqi, born Adnan latif Hamid al-Sweidawi, serves as the Head of Military Shura or the Military Council. Al-Iraqi was one of the Ba'athist loyalists who were imprisoned in Camp Bucca. After spending three years in the camp, being released in 2010, al-Iraqi went to Syria where he later led the ISIS forces in Aleppo and Idlib. The senior ISIL commander is accused of assassinating prominent members of the Free Syrian Army.

Abu Omar al-Shishani

The Field Commander of the jihadist group is Abu Omar al-Shishani, known before as Tarkhan Tayumurazovich. Al-Shishani was born in Georgis and was even a veteran fighter of the Georgian Land Forces. He was discharged from the Georgian Army after which he turned into a jihadist.

Abu Muhammad al-Adnani

The Spokesman for the Islamic state is Abu Muhammad al-Adnani who was born in 1977 as Taha Subhi Falaha. He was also imprisoned for some time and was released in 2010. Al-Adnani is known as well for his 'Indeed Your Lord Is Ever Watchful' speech in which he instructed supporters to "kill a disbelieving American or European" "in any manner or way however it may be."

Chapter 4 Brutal Propaganda

ISIS has been known as one of the most brutal and radical Islamic jihadists ever. Their twisted interpretation of the Quran and the Muslim religion in general is the main reason why the group has resorted in actions too violent for one to stomach. Among the methods of establishing fear and proving their strength is the use of propaganda. The videotaped executions of numerous innocent lives are just some of the brutal propaganda materials that the group employs.

James Wright Foley

James Foley was an American journalist who worked for GlobalPost, a news organization. He was the first victim of ISIS cruelty that has been videotaped and showed for everyone to see. In the video that showed Foley's execution, the masked terrorist proclaimed, as if talking to the US President himself, that "Today your military air force has attacked us daily... Your strikes have caused casualties amongst Muslims,"

Jim, as he was fondly called, grew up in Illinois and New Hampshire in the United States. A 1996 graduate from the Marquette University, Foley was also an alumnus of the University of Massachusetts Amherst and the Northwestern University. After earning degrees in journalism and other related fields, Foley joined Teach For America (TFA) where he taught in Arizona, Illinois, and Massachusetts.

He moved on to join some projects in Baghdad that were funded by USAID. These projects aimed to help Iraq rebuild its civil service. Foley later became an embedded journalist accompanying the American troops in Iraq. In 2011, he was assigned to cover Afghanistan after he joined *Stars and Stripes*, an American newspaper that focused on the Armed Forces of the United States. In April of the same year, Foley who was now working with GlobalPost and covering the uprising against Libyan ruler Muammar al-Gaddafi, was taken hostage along with freelance reporter Clare Morgana Gillis, and Manu Brabo, a photographer from Spain.

It was also during their capture that photojournalist Anton Hammerl was killed. Gaddafi loyalists were responsible for the death of Hammerl and the detainment of Foley and the other journalists. The captives were released after 44 days but that won't signify the end of Foley's misfortunes.

James Foley was still working for GlobalPost when he was again abducted this time with John Cantlie, a British journalist. They, along with a translator were riding a taxi when they were stopped somewhere between northwestern Syria and the Turkish border. This happened on November 2012, a few months before Cantlie himself was kidnapped and rescued. It is believed that the group was

Foley's mother, who identified his son in the video which the terrorists entitled "A Message to America", proclaimed his son to be a hero of some sort for helping people everywhere to open their eyes to the atrocities done by this militant group especially against the Syrians. She said the whole family is so proud of her son who sacrificed himself for the benefit of others.

Steven Joel Sotloff

American journalist and *Time Magazine* contributor Steven Sotloff was included in the propaganda video that showed the execution of fellow journalist James Foley. In the video, the masked murderer, after taking Foley's life with a slash to his neck, threatened Sotloff's life with the words, "The life of this American citizen, Obama, depends on your next decision". True to their words, Sotloff was beheaded sometime before the release of the video showing his death at the hands of his captors on September 2, 2014.

Sotloff is also an Israeli citizen who also happens to be a grandson of one of the survivors of the Holocaust. The Pinecrest, Florida native worked for a number of news magazines aside from *Time* most of the time in foreign lands such as Libya, Egypt and Turkey. But it was his work in Aleppo, Syria that would prove deadly. Sotloff was abducted on August 4, 2013 along with his fixer and the latter's family. They were later released but Sotloff remained a prisoner of the terrorists.

David Cawthorne Haines

At the end of the "A Second Message to America" video that featured Sotloff's beheading, humanitarian aid worker David Haines was shown. Like the first video, Haines' life was threatened if the US government and other coalition forces did not stop their attack against ISIS. Haines was beheaded on September 13, 2014 which was shown in the video, "A Message to the Allies of Amewrica".

Alan Henning

Another humanitarian aid worker, British Alan Henning was beheaded by ISIS. Henning was in Al-Dana in Syria when the terrorist forces took over the city. He was shown at the end of David Haines' execution video and was later beheaded in another video released on October 3, 2014.

Peter Edward Kassig

Peter Kassig, later known as Abdul-Rahman Kassig, was doing humanitarian aid when he was captured in Eastern Syria. During his captivity, Kassig converted to Islam which explains the change in name. Kassig shared cells with other foreign captives including John Cantlie and Nicolas Henin, who described

Kassig as sincere in his conversion to Islam. Kassig was threatened in the latter part of the Henning beheading video. The threat was consummated as seen in another video released on November 16, 2014.

Syrian Soldiers

Eighteen captured members of the Syrian Army were also shown beheaded in Peter Kassig's execution video. Their death was branded one of the most gruesome among all the videoed beheadings released by ISIS.

Battle of Arsal Beheadings

Ali Al-Sayyed was a sergeant with the Lebanese Army when he was captured by ISIL forces during the Battle of Arsal. Images of his execution were posted on Twitter by an ISIL member, identified as Abu Musaab Hafid al-Baghdadi. Another Lebanese soldier imprisoned during the Battle of Arsal, Abbas Medlej, was also beheaded by his captors. Rumors state that Medlej tried to escape but was captrured and executed. His execution added to the anger of the Lebanese people after pictures of his gruesome end were posted online.

Hervé Gourdel

Hervé Gourdel was hiking in Algeria's Djurdjura National Park when he was abducted by ISIS forces in the country. A video released by the abductors insisted that the French government cease airstrikes if they wish to see Gourdel, a French mountaineering guide, alive. Sadly, Gourdel was beheaded on September 24, 2014.

Kenji Goto and Haruna Yukawa

Japanese Haruna Yukawa was captured by the FSA in Syria in April 2014. He was granted his release after journalist Kenji Goto acted as his interpreter. Both men went back to Japan but returned to Syria for different reasons. They were captured and were shown in a video where ISIS forces demanded $200 million from the Japanese government and the release of five jihadist inmates. The duo was later beheaded as shown in separate videos released.

Muath "Moaz" al-Kaseasbeh

The latest move by ISIS to cause a major uproar was the execution of a captured Royal Jordanian Air Force pilot. Lt. Muath al-Kaseasbeh crashed over Syria during an airstrike conducted by coalition forces. Al-Kaseasbeh can be seen in the video "Healing the Believers' Chests", locked in a cage being doused in gasoline and later burned to death.

In retaliation, the Jordanian government executed two ISIS jihadists that the terrorist group previously wanted released. Sajida al-Rishawi, an al-Qaeda suicide bomber, was one of the inmates that ISIS wanted freed in return for the release of Kenji Goto. The execution was done just hours after Jordan learned of their pilot's death. Like a father who recently lost a son in a tragic and evil manner, King Abdullah ibn al-Hussein vowed that they will "crush the terrorist group" "till (they) run out of fuel and bullets". To show the terrorists how serious the 'warrior king' is, the former military man himself will lead the bombing mission against the Islamic State group. His 35 years of experience in the military as a pilot will sure come in handy against the ISIS.

Instead of instilling fear, ISIS has succeeded in doing the opposite. Muslims who have stayed silent are now voicing their grievances and condemnation for ISIS' actions.

Nicolas Henin escaped the same fate as those mentioned above. The French journalist was also taken hostage by ISIS but had the fortune of being released in April 2014. Among his cellmates during his captivity were Foley, Sotloff, Haines, and Henning. As he mentioned during an interview after his release, "Normally when you are released you are free - I'm not." He went on to describe his experience as "very brutal."

Chapter 5 The Treatment of Women And Children Under ISIS

All throughout history, innocent lives have been caught in the crossfire of violent conflicts many of them women and children.

An American woman who disappeared in August 2013 was later revealed to be held hostage by ISIS. Kayla Jean Mueller, a humanitarian worker who worked with Support to Life and the Danish Refugee Council, was stationed in Turkey to provide aid to Syrian refugees displaced by war. Before that, the Northern Arizona University graduate spent time in India, Israel and other parts of the world in her quest to "not let (this) suffering be normal". She was first reported to be with the group Doctors Without Borders (MSF) when she was abducted. While not actually working for the MSF, according to the group's official statement, Mueller was there to accompany a technician who worked on an MSF hospital located in Aleppo, Syria. The duo stayed overnight in Aleppo and was abducted on their way to a bus station the following day. The Islamic State put the ransom for the Prescott, Arizona native at $6.6 million. However, any further moves to get Mueller safely back on American shores may come a bit too late as ISIS recently released a statement along with a photograph saying the 26-year old Mueller has perished after an airstrike conducted by the coalition. ISIS claims that Mueller was inside a building in Raqqa, the Islamic State capital, when it was felled during the airstrike.

Steps are currently being undertaken to verify this claim. However, many are casting doubts to this as ISIS has yet to produce evidence aside from a photograph of the collapsed building. Some has even displaced this as a PR stunt by the group.

The atrocities against women do not end with Mueller. Scores of innocent women are being subjected to torture, rape and humiliation each day that passes. The Islamist terrorists defend their actions by saying all these were justified by God and they laid out all the rules in a pamphlet that armed men distributed in Mosul, Iraq in December, 2014. The pamphlet, entitled "Questions and Answers on Female Slaves and their Freedom" were met with shock and disbelief. Sadly, those in Mosul who first read the pamphlet had the same thought -- there was nothing they can do.

The Islamist militant group argued that non-believers, particularly the women, can be captured and made into slaves. Women can be bought, traded or given as gifts. Yazidi women, in particular, are said to be "treated like cattle". The pamphlet also takes into account sexual intercourse with slaves. It goes on to say that the Quran allows the owner to have intercourse with his slave immediately upon purchase if she was a virgin. Female slaves who were no longer virgins were allowed to have their uterus "purified" before having intercourse. This simply means the owner should wait for the female slave to have her period first before having sex with her. This, according to the terrorists, is an indication that she is pure or not pregnant. Female slaves who haven't reached puberty yet can also be raped as long as she is "fit for intercourse". If the girl is deemed not fit for intercourse, the owner can still do what he wishes sans actual intercourse.

New reports indicate that the terrorist group has turned to innocent children in their efforts to strike fear in everybody's hearts. While a certain level of fear will always be there, the latest actions of ISIS may trigger more hatred against them, even much worse than what resulted from the burning of the Jordanian pilot. ISIS has resorted to giving children guns to help their cause. Even those as young as 8 years old are being trained to be part of their militant group.

The United Nations have also reported that ISIS is selling children as slaves. There are also reports that children in the war-torn areas occupied by ISIS are subjected to rape and crucifixion. Even worse, many have been executed by beheading and being buried alive among other barbaric ways. The militant group is also using mentally-challenged youngsters to further their campaign of terror. Such children are being strapped with explosives without them knowing or understanding anything that is going on. One can just imagine the horror of using mentally-challenged children as suicide bombers. In response to this knowledge, the United Nations particularly Renate Winter of the U.N. Committee on the Rights of the

Child, has encouraged everyone to put premium on the lives of children in the war-ravaged areas.

Chapter 6. Why ISIS Is Thriving

Even after the wrath of the many voices that have been raised against ISIS and their wrongdoings, some people still find the militant group attractive. With every hundred that wither in disgust at their actions, there are a few who are drawn to them. This makes one wonder how the group seem to be swelling in number even after numerous attacks on their line.

Even some Americans in the United States are being swayed to the cause of ISIS. In the "Flames of War" propaganda video released by the jihadist group, one masked terrorist was speaking in English and Arabic. This led American authorities to believe that he may be one of theirs. In the video, the English-speaking man oversaw the executions of Syrian soldiers whom he called kuffar or non-Muslims and who were first forced to dig their own graves. The US Federal Bureau of Investigation took it upon itself to identify the man with a North American-like accent. Another masked militant who is fluent in English and is featured prominently in other gruesome execution videos has been identified according to the FBI Director James Comey. This man appeared in most of the propaganda videos that saw Western hostages executed brutally, particularly Americans James Foley and Steven Sotloff, and British David Haines. The use of an English-speaking Muslim was a way for the militant group to persuade other Westerners to believe in their cause and possibly recruit them. With the number of

Americans and other Westerners trying to join the group, their propaganda could be working.

Proof of such is the three American teenaged girls who wanted and tried to join the radical group. The three youngsters, all hailing from Denver, were arrested in Frankfurt, Germany and brought back to their homeland. The girls, aged 16 and younger, were supposed to meet an ISIS personality in Germany who were tasked to help them reach Syria and become part of their cause. But these three girls weren't the first Americans to fall under the trap of ISIS.

Shannon Maureen Conley of Colorado was a clueless teenager with a big mouth. This is how her own mother, AnaMaria, described the younger Conley after learning of her arrest. The nineteen-year old converted to Islam and was later radicalized probably after meeting a Syrian ISIS member online. Conley changed her name to Halima then to Amatullah which meant "servant of Allah" and planned to marry the man she met on the Internet. A certified nurse's aide, Conley was supposed to work as a nurse for the militant group. She is now serving a four-year jail term.

Western women have been a prime target for the recruiting efforts of ISIS. The group has been publishing a magazine called al-Shamika. Also called the "Jihad Cosmo", the magazine may have been instrumental in persuading three Minnesota women to leave the country to become part of ISIS. Reports say that around 130 women have been successfully recruited by ISIS through the help of their magazine along with other forms of media. Another method of recruitment by ISIS is promising the women money in exchange for getting impregnated by a jihadi militant. Women who join the group are not required to join the men in the field. They are, however, expected to cook and clean for the militants.

Another radicalized American, Adam Dandach has admitted to planning to join the terrorist group after he was arrested by the FBI. The twenty-year-old Fadi Fadi, as he was called, was arrested at the John Wayne Airport in Los Angeles, after the authorities identified him as a potential risk. The Orange County resident falsified his passport in order to travel to Turkey, reports said.

Nineteen-year old Mohammed Hamzah Khan was also arrested for planning to join ISIS. The youngster from Illinois was taken at the O'Hare airport in Chicago as he was about to fly to Turkey via Vienna. Upon learning of his arrest, relatives and friends of the Khan family were surprised with the development since they've known the Khan as a nice and polite young man.

Donald Ray Morgan is another American accused of trying to aid the militant group. The 44-year old from North Carolina was arrested at the JFK Airport after it was discovered that he sold a gun at the online gun-selling site called Carolina Shooters Club. While he was arrested because he was not allowed to possess a gun thanks to a previous conviction, Morgan was already on the watch list of the US government. Calling himself Abu Omar al Amreeki, Morgan tweeted his allegiance to ISIS by posting, "Mujahid pledging allegiance to Abu Bakr al-Baghdadi and Islamic State commanding good and forbidding evil." Other tweets by the former bodybuilding champ, revealed his intention to join ISIS including the one where he stated, "To the brothers inside Syria and Iraq be humble and grateful many of us are trying to come as some are arrested and others delayed."

Since the release of the propaganda videos and the concern of dealing with an American ISIS member, the United States government has intensified their drive to prevent others from joining the terrorist group. They have also estimated that at least 100 Americans have joined and fought for ISIS. At least twelve of them have been identified by the authorities.

As mentioned, ISIS is starting to get supporters from other Western countries not only the United States. Another tweet posted on the popular social networking site Twitter showed a young boy holding a severed head. The boy is a son of a former Australian convict who found his way to Syria and in the arms of the ISIS. Khaled Sharrouf was convicted for taking part in planned attacks on Melbourne and Sydney. But after four years in prison, Sharrouf was released and is now in Syria after using his brother's passport to leave Australia.

Salma and Zahra Halane of Manchester are two more Westerners who are probably in Syria right now after pledging their allegiance to ISIS. The British sisters are believed to have married into ISIS and may be pregnant with so-called future mujahideen or warriors. The two were training to be doctors back in their homeland.

The now infamous Jihadi Jane claimed she is a citizen of the United Kingdom, or used to be. She was responsible for posting an image of James Foley being executed which came with a caption that said, "If this doesn't bring a bit comfort and ease to your heart then #checkyourself." The mysterious Twitter user who some believe hailed from Canada also calls herself Lama Sharif al-Shammari. Some reports say that the woman behind Jihadi Jane may be one of the women running brothels with Yazidi women as sex slaves.

Another British woman who has been proven to be a member of the jihadist group is Sally Jones who now goes by Sakinah Hussain. Jones is the one who posted a Twitter rant that talked about beheading Christians with a blunt knife. Jones used to play lead guitars for Krunch, an all-girl rock band based in the South East during the 1990s. After meeting hacker Junaid Hussain, the mother of two converted to Islam and later became a radical. Hussain, who hails from Birmingham, Alabama, and Jones are now married and based in Syria fighting for the ISIS. It is also believed that Jones brought along youngest son, a ten-year old boy from a previous relationship.

A couple of Austrian teenagers have also been recruited and are now in Syria. Fifteen-year old

Sabina Selimovic and sixteen-year old Samra Kesinovic are said to have fallen for the "cash-for-babies" recruitment scheme of ISIS that was mentioned earlier. The two teeners reportedly told their friends that they were both alive and pregnant. While this bit of news cannot be verified, authorities are sure that the two have married Chechen militants.

Most of the recruiting efforts of the jihadists are focused on young people, particularly women. Like sexual predators, ISIS are prancing on the young people's naiveté with the promise of providing honor to the cause either by fighting those who are against their belief or by giving birth to future warriors of their faith.